# Undelivered letters to her

## Midnight Pharaoh

(Smiley)

To the one who poured life into my heart
with a single *smile*.
To the one who makes my heart sing.

To, the *lovely*, her…

## <u>If only</u>

*If only
you could see yourself
through my eyes.*

*You would understand why.*

## *Fall for you*

*It's everything you say
and everything you do
that made me fall for you.*

## <u>We'll never grow apart</u>

*Drown me in your eyes.*
*Dip me in your heart.*
*Wash me with your tenderness.*
*We'll never grow apart.*

## <u>You deserve to be loved</u>

*You deserve to be loved,*
*Taken care of,*
*Treated right,*
*And showered with affection.*

*5.6.22*

### *I'm still falling*

*If I say that I fell for you*
*I would be lying*
*Because darling!*
*I'm still falling.*

*8.6.22*

### <u>The ways I once knew</u>

*You've reminded me
of how to feel again
in all the ways
I've forgotten
I once knew.*

*7.6.22*

## <u>*Flashbacks*</u>

*To the tenderness of*
*your kisses on my neck.*

*To the taste of*
*your lips on mine.*

*To the touch of your fingers*
*caressing my arm.*

*To my fingers sailing softly*
*between every strand of your golden hair.*

*To your magical*
*bright blue eyes.*

*13.6.22*

## To the 'lovely' you

*I woke up with a smile,*
*I wish you did too.*
*May your day be special,*
*as so are you.*
*To the lovely you*
*with the lovely smile.*
*May you always be happy,*
*not just for a while.*

*5.6.22*

## *I'll win the whole race*

*From the first time
I saw your face,
you made my heart and mind
fly to space.
That's when I realized
that you're the one to chase.
And if you want a champion,
I'll win the whole race.*

### *I'll be your wonderland.*

*I'll buy you flowers
and hold your hand.
Walk with you on the beach,
Draw hearts in the sand.
You want to tell me something?
I'll listen and understand.
And if you want a fairy-tale,
I'll be your wonderland.*

### *If I have to, I will*

*If I have to*
*sail through storms,*
*walk over fire,*
*fight every wave,*
*dive into the unknown,*

*..*
*I will still be there*
*For you*

## <u>Something about your eyes</u>

*There's something about your eyes,
makes me fall for you
and makes me realize
that what I'm looking for
is here beside me.*

## <u>Hand in hand again</u>

*Standing in the rain
side by side and
hand in hand again,
it's hard to explain
but it's so perfect.*

## <u>As I look into your eyes</u>

*As I look into your eyes,*
*I could see countless stars*
*pouring down into my heart,*
*splashing melodies out to the world,*
*And settling in the endless*
*night sky,*
*brightening up my world.*

## <u>Sometimes!</u>

*Sometimes*
*the hardest thing in life*
*is wanting to be in love with someone*
*who wants to be*
*in love with you.*

## <u>*For eternity*</u>

*I want to capture
the smell of your perfume,
frame it,
And hang it
on the walls of my heart
for eternity.*

## <u>Along came you</u>

*In a world where love is hard to come by...*
*In a world where it's common to get hurt and cry...*
*In a world full of farewell, so long and goodbye...*
*You came along and showed me, it's worth it*
*to still try...*

## *I close my eyes*

*I close my eyes*
*and I still see*
*you.*

## <u>*I'll be right there*</u>

*No matter how hard*
*Life pulls you back*
*I'll be right there*
*Pulling you in my arms,*
*Telling you*

*To continue*
*Being your strong self.*

### <u>I carry your love</u>

*When I look into your eyes*
*There is an essence*
*That lifts up my whole being*

*Leaves me cradled*
*In that warm scent you carry*

*As I carry your love*
*In my heart.*

## <u>The thought of you</u>

*Even when I'm down,*
*laying in my bed,*
*drowning in my thoughts*
*and almost giving up,*

*The thought of you*
*and the little messages*
*you send me,*
*keep me going.*

## The 'Why'

*Last night I had a dream.*

*In another universe,*
*We are hand in hand,*
*Looking through a portal*
*At the 'me & you' now*
*Being far apart*
*And wondering...*
*'Why!'*

### <u>That happy</u>

*Her: "How is it being close to me?"*

*Me: "It's like a piece of heaven fell inside my heart. Yes, that happy."*

*26.03.22*

## *The way you...*

*The way you smile when I hold you close,*
*The way you laugh when I tell a joke,*
*The way you bite your lips looking at me,*
*Make me want you more.*

## *If I miss the stars*

*If I miss the stars,*
*I just look at*
*the sparkle in your eyes.*

### <u>Well, because I told them</u>

*Tonight,*
*the stars,*
*the moon, and the skies*
*know about you.*

*Well, because I told them.*

## <u>The sum of me</u>

*Darling,*

*Like You,*
*I want someone*
*who will want*
*the sum of me.*
*Not just some of me.*

### *Just to be loved enough*

*A beautiful heart*
*With a beautiful love*
*Sent down to earth*
*From the heavens above*
*Doesn't want too much*
*Just to be loved enough*

## <u>*Remembering*</u>

*It's not about
Forgetting,
It's about being ok
remembering.*

### *It's just a dream*

*I used to think
that you can only dream
in your sleep.
Until I met you.
Now I'm dreaming all the time.
But it's just a dream.*

## <u>Yes. But.</u>

*Right person*
*Right place*
*Right time*
*But*
*Without the effort*
*And understanding,*
*Without the determination*
*And courage,*
*Without the caring, respect*
*And the listening*
*The 3 rights*
*Could disappear.*

### *The smile that's got your name*

*When, out of nowhere,*
*You appear,*
*My whole body, face, and mind freeze*
*just to absorb the fact*
*that I've just seen you.*
*That's when that smile appears*
*on my face.*
*The smile that's got your name*
*Written all over it.*

## <u>Your existence</u>

*Your existence*
*fills my existence*
*with such happiness.*

## *I did not know*

*I never knew*
*I wanted a life*
*before I was born.*

*I never knew*
*I needed love*
*before I met you.*

## *I was reborn*

*Do you want to know
what you have done
to my whole being when I met you?*

*It felt like it was
'The first day of my life'*

*I was reborn.
Full of hope, life, and love.*

## <u>The first and the last</u>

*There are 7 billion people in the world*
*and you're still the first on my mind each morning*
*and the last on my mind before I fall asleep.*

## *It wasn't just life*

*It wasn't just life
that you have woken up
in my heart.*

*It was my heart
itself.*

## *You're in every cell of my being*

*You are in every cell*
*of my whole being.*
*My conscious, my subconscious,*
*my heart, My emotions,*
*my heartbeats,*
*my mind, my thoughts,*
*my eyes, my tears,*
*my purpose, my goals,*
*my mornings, my afternoons, my evenings,*
*my nights, my dreams*
*you have me in your*
*gravitational power like*
*the sun has the earth.*

*you have me in your hands*
*like an ocean holds water,*
*you have me more than all that.*
*You have me and you will always have me.*

## <u>No matter what I write</u>

*No matter what I write*
*or how much I write*
*about you,*
*it will never be enough.*

*You deserve a whole*
*new alphabet.*

## *The poetry itself*

*Poems,*
*songs,*
*words,*
*thoughts,*
*all do not do you*
*justice*
*when you are*
*the poetry*
*itself.*

## <u>You still make me smile</u>

*Even when you're
not around, you still
make me smile.*

## *<u>Falling for your you</u>*

*People talk about
the beauty on the outside
and the beauty
on the inside.
But, Darling,
you got both.*

*My me
loves the idea
of falling
for your you!*

### You make me love me

*When you talk to me,*
*when you sit next to me,*
*when you sing with me,*
*& Just by telling me*
*about me.*

*you make me love me,*

*Now that's a lot of me*
*coming from you.*

*So, my me is appreciating*
*your you!*

### <u>All I needed to know</u>

*Seeing you,*
*talking to you,*
*laughing with you,*
*is there any other emotional*
*pleasure?!*

*Your you*
*is all I needed to know*
*about you.*

*And darling,*
*your 'you' is enough.*

## <u>*Selfie*</u>

*I want
to
be
the
moments
that make you forget
to
take
a
selfie.*

### <u>*Every. Time.*</u>

*Every time*
*we hug,*
*I never want*
*to let go.*
*I just have to.*

*Every time*
*you are next to me,*
*I never want*
*you to go.*
*You just have to.*

## <u>My ticket to heaven</u>

*Your smile*
*is the light to my darkness.*
*Your laugh*
*is the music to my ears.*
*Your eyes*
*are the stars to my sky.*
*Your words*
*Are the path to my happiness.*

*And your soul*
*is my ticket to heaven.*

### *Just to hold you, dear!*

*I want you here*
*I need you here*
*I'll do anything*
*just to hold you, dear!*

*a chance to love you*
*a chance to show you*
*my love for you*
*that's got no fear.*

*you're in my heart*
*you're in my mind*
*you've got me captivated*
*whether you're far or near.*

*I'll do anything*
*just to hold you, dear!*

### <u>*I know you're out there*</u>

*Yes, I've stopped the search*
*but I still deeply care.*

*with a heart full of love*
*that I'm not afraid to share.*

*"In your existence I believe."*
*- said the smile that I wear.*

*Not sure where you are*
*but I know you're out there.*

### <u>There isn't another you</u>

*You always tell me
there is someone for me
out there.*

*But, love!
How could it be
when there isn't another
you?*

## <u>And dreaming of you</u>

*Thinking of you*
*going to sleep,*

*thinking of you*
*waking up*

*and dreaming of you*
*in-between.*

## <u>I have</u>

*And I have finally*
*Found home*

*In your eyes.*

## <u>When I am asked</u>

*When I am asked*
*about where I would want to be,*

*I always think of your arms.*

## <u>The light at the end</u>

*I always heard about
the light
at the end of the tunnel.*

*But didn't believe it
until I have met you.*

## <u>No longer lost at sea</u>

*By the look in her eyes,*
*By the touch of her hand,*
*And by the smile on her face*
*I came to understand*
*I'm no longer lost at sea*
*I have found my shore,*
*I have found my land.*

## Intoxicated

*I remain to this day
intoxicated on our first kiss.
The kiss that sent warmth
flying through my veins.
The kiss that got my heart
pounding so hard,
it almost jumped out of my chest.*

*I remain to this day
intoxicated on the taste
of your tender lips.*

*16.6.22*

## Her Kiss

*She kissed me like*
*the sun kisses*
*the ocean.*

*And she hugged me like*
*the night skies*
*hugs the moon.*

*4.7.22*

## *To you,*

*Even though there are these walls that you've
built high enough for no one to reach
and hurt that tender kind heart of yours,*

*Even though there are others who are
cluelessly and mindlessly trying to climb
these endless walls,*

*I choose to speak to your soul instead.
I choose to caress your heart instead and listen to
every whisper and every word.*

*And take each day as it comes.*

*Maybe one day your heart will see it clearly
and come outside of these walls and greet my heart
and pour life into my soul as you've poured life into my heart.*

*Maybe one day we will look at each other and think
Have we been missing all that?*

*I know I have.*

## <u>To everyone who hurt you,</u>

*They never realized the uniqueness of your soul and of who you are.*
*They never thought that what they had was/is*
*someone else's long lost dream*
*for which they are willing to do the impossible.*
*They never realized what they'd done to the way you now look at*
*life.*

*I may be too late, but I'm here now with the intention of staying.*
*Even if your thoughts sometimes take over and send you to*
*that dark place in your mind where all the memories of*
*the pain and mistreatments are,*
*I will still be here for you.*
*Letting you know how special you are*
*even if you don't believe it.*

*Letting you know when you're missed.*
*Bringing back your smile to your beautiful face*
*when the smile cannot be seen.*
*Holding you in my arms and telling you that*
*You are more than enough.*

*My darling,*
*I am here now.*

## Let me be yours

*All I want you to do is to*
*take a stroll inside my heart,*
*take a look around,*
*feel every corner.*

*And, if you like what you see,*
*if you feel what I feel,*
*you are welcome to stay and*
*claim this heart to be yours*
*forever.*

*Do not be afraid to let go of your fear.*
*This heart has got so much love to give*
*and so much care.*
*This heart knows how to deal with a heart like yours.*
*A heart so big, a heart so kind, yet so fragile.*

*We have only got one life*
*and if this means that I am taking the risk*
*by letting you in,*
*then I would gladly take that risk.*

*Pop in for a visit inside my heart.*
*You never know, you might not want to leave.*
*You never know.*

*Let me show you the love you have been*
*Wanting and needing for a long time.*

*Let me show you the love*
*That you deserve.*

*Let me be*
*yours.*

## <u>What broke your heart so bad?</u>

*I want to know what broke your heart so bad? that you decided to build these walls around your heart so high, that you promised yourself to never ever let anyone in and to never fall in love again to a point where you don't believe in love anymore.*

*What broke your heart so bad?*

### How would you know

*And how would you know.*
*Unless you let things flow.*
*And whenever you freeze.*
*Just remember to breathe.*

*30.6.22*

## A 'happy ever after'

To me, a happy ever after is no longer a wedding ring.
To me, a happy ever after is the song that we sing.
To me, a happy ever after is forever in your arms.
To me, a happy ever after is forever holding hands.
To me, a happy ever after is the smile on your face.
To me, a happy ever after is no longer a race.

You see, a happy ever after
is living every moment with you.
It's the hug when we don't want to ever let go.
It's the kiss that we steal,
and the rush that we feel.

You see, a happy ever after
is taking care of your heart.
It's listening to your every whisper,
and every word, my sweetheart.

You see, a happy ever after
is our language that only we can understand.
It's the comfort that I feel
from the touch of your hand.
It's the jokes that we make.
It's staying up all night wide awake.

*You see, a happy ever after*
*is a 2-sugar coffee every morning together.*
*It's the snuggle under the cover*
*in a rainy cold weather.*
*It's the sound of your laughter*
*that makes it all a lot better.*

*Baby, a 'happy ever after'*
*is you*
*and me together.*

*22.6.22*

### A forever with you

*If we ever meet again
in another world
and another life,
I want you to hold me firmly
and never let go
for I want a forever with you.*

*25.6.22*

## When I miss you,

*When I miss you,*
*I look at the*
*image of you*
*inside my heart.*


*15.7.22*

## *I was home*

*Back to the four walls of my room*
*where supposedly I'm home*
*the sound of my thoughts*
*echoes inside my heart*
*setting fire to my chest.*
*How can this be home?*

*The truth is*
*I was home*
*when my head was resting on your chest.*
*I was home between your arms*
*I was home with you*
*breathing the blueness of your eyes.*
*I was home.*

*Now I'm here again all alone.*
*Fire burning through my veins.*

*If you only knew.*

*I wish you could have taken my heart*
*and given it a home.*

*As I wish you were – forever –*
*My home.*

*25.6.22*

## *The idea of me and you*

*You've been hurt many times,*
*believe me, so have I.*
*You're terrified as much as me,*
*but we've got to try.*

*We're both too scared and overwhelmed,*
*and that's ok.*
*Let's look into each other's eyes,*
*and take it day by day*

*I'll take you in my arms and*
*whisper: "we're good together."*
*I'll kiss your forehead and tell you,*
*it will only get better.*

*It's too good to be true, I know,*
*yet it is so true.*
*How can we ignore the greatness of*
*the idea of me and you.*

*6.7.22*

## <u>No one came close</u>

*Trust me when I say*
*that no one else came*
*even close.*
*You are everything*
*I only dreamed*
*to, one day, have.*


*17.7.22*

## <u>On my mind</u>

*Here is a list of what I've been thinking about
since I opened my eyes this morning:*

- *You.*

*16.7.22*

## <u>Surreal to real</u>

*Our surreal world together,*
*Just got real.*

*And what a beautiful reality*
*This is.*


*17.7.22*

## The stars

*I would rather*
*follow the flow of the stars.*
*than try to rewrite them.*
*Afterall,*
*they have brought us together.*
*And that is the best thing*
*the stars have ever done*
*for me.*

*17.7.22*

### <u>*Giving you my world*</u>

*I wouldn't have
promised you
the stars,
if I wasn't willing to
give you my
whole world.*

*17.7.22*

## <u>Just the thought</u>

*Just the thought
of a few moments
spent with you,
fills my entire being
with an overflowing,
everlasting
happiness.*

*19.7.22*

## <u>When I see you</u>

*When I see you,*
*I instantly forget my worry.*
*And things become so clear,*
*Same things that were once blurry.*

*Even my doubts and everything I fear,*
*they're like never existed,*
*and all of a sudden disappear.*

*Even when I'm down*
*and my mind is playing games,*
*A look in your eyes*
*And in the facts, my mind remains.*

*The fact that I love you*
*And I know you love me too.*
*Whether or not you'll ever say it,*
*I just know you do.*

## <u>And it hurts</u>

*And it hurts,*
*Because*
*You mean something.*

*4.8.22*

## <u>Were</u>

*I miss the days*
*where you and I were*
*seeing eye to eye*
*into our souls.*

*I miss the moments*
*where me and you*
*were one not two*
*and losing control.*

### <u>How could I?</u>

*And how could I
go another day,
without your smile
that makes it all ok.*

*I want to hold you close
baby, if I may,
for one last time
before you walk away.*

## *I lose myself*

*And in the loneliness of my thoughts*
*and the waves of emotions within*
*I lost myself.*
*Almost seems as if I always fall*
*for the unreachable*
*and the impossible.*

*Almost seems as if I always fall*
*For what I know I'll lose.*

*In the lonesome of me,*
*I lose myself.*

## *The day will come, and I won't cope*

*Stuck between*
*I can't lose you and*
*knowing the day will come.*

*Stuck between*
*a mind that knows and*
*a heart not willing to let go.*

*Stuck between*
*Our first hello and*
*our inevitable goodbye.*

*It took me a long time to find you.*
*Now I'm scared of losing you.*

*One thing is certain.*
*The day will come*
*and I won't cope.*

*3.7.22 – 11:59*

### The end

*And as life itself*
*everything else*
*always comes to*
*an end.*

*Saturday 6.8.22 – 23:59*

### *Isn't that a reason to?*

*You said that*
*you couldn't hide your feelings*
*even if you wanted to.*

*Isn't that, my dear,*
*a good enough reason for you?*

*To take the risk,*
*to fight your fears,*
*And to go with what you know*
*to be true?*

*9.8.22 – 11:00*

### *Thinking about you*

*Between the trees*
*and the fresh air,*

*That nice breeze*
*that used to touch your hair,*

*I sit here silently,*
*thinking about you.*

*The way you smile*
*and everything you do.*

*9.8.22 – 21:15*

## <u>Welcome back</u>

*Welcome back to my arms,*
*And I welcome myself to yours.*

*Welcome back to us, my love!*

*10.8.22*

## *She asked*

*Her: "I know how you feel about me. I see it in every look you give me. I see it in every word and every action. I feel it when we hug. But I want to hear it from you."*

*Me: "Darling, I want to say that - to me - you are life, but the fact is you are more than that. You are everything I dreamed of. you are every characteristic I was looking for. You are the shy that can be wild. You are the kind that can be hard if needed be. You are the smile that changes how I see life, you are the comfort and the home when I'm lost.*
*You are the warmth in the cold. You are the happy beyond happy. You are you. And that, my darling, is way more than enough for me to fall for you.*
*My every action and emotion are simply controlled by the simplest look on your heavenly face."*

## <u>My everything</u>

*Baby,*

*You will always be*

*my everything,*

*my whole world,*

*and my entire universe.*

*10.8.22 - ∞*

## <u>You always make me smile</u>

*You always
manage to
make me smile,
even on
my worst days.*

## <u>*Eternity*</u>

*Someone asked me today*
*if I believed in eternity.*

*I smiled, and said:*

*"Yes. I see it every time*
*I look into her eyes."*

*17.8.22*

## I fell in love with

*I fell in love with*
*who you are, and*
*everything that you are.*

*I fell in love with*
*you*
*for so many reasons.*

*You made me feel again after*
*being numb for so long.*

*I fell in love with*
*your soul.*

*I fell in love with*
*your voice, your laugh*
*your smile,*
*and how your smile compliments*
*that sparkle in your eyes.*

*I fell in love with*
*the idea of you that became life itself.*

*I fell in love with*
*the idea of us.*

*I fell in love,*
*and I'm still falling*
*for you.*

*16.8.22*

## <u>*You are my heaven*</u>

*I look at her, and*
*I don't take my eyes off her.*

*"Why are you looking at me like that?"*
 - *She asked with a smile on her face.*

*"There is nothing more beautiful in the world."*
 - *I replied while stroking her hair.*
*"And heaven isn't far anymore now, my love!"*
 - *I continued as I kissed her forehead.*

*I will never have enough of looking at your face.*

*That's when I feel peace, comfort, happiness, and love*
*flowing through my body and mind.*

*You are my heaven.*

*Instagram:*
*@MidnightPharaoh*

Printed in Great Britain
by Amazon

19215786R00058